Star Trackers

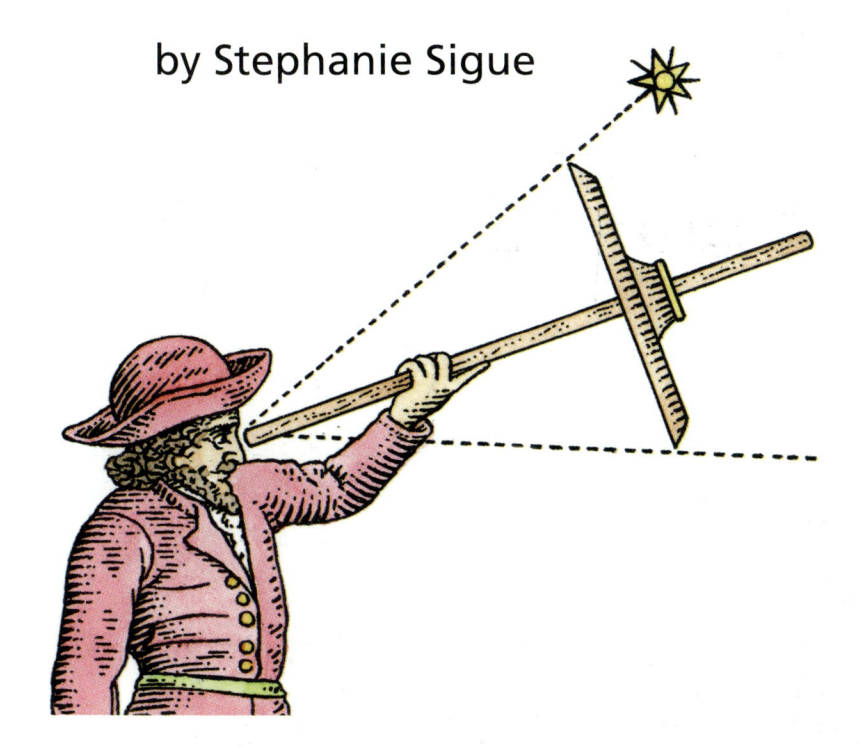

by Stephanie Sigue

Scott Foresman is an imprint of

PEARSON

Glenview, Illinois • Boston, Massachusetts • Mesa, Arizona
Shoreview, Minnesota • Upper Saddle River, New Jersey

Photographs

Every effort has been made to secure permission and provide appropriate credit for photographic material. The publisher deeply regrets any omission and pledges to correct errors called to its attention in subsequent editions.

Unless otherwise acknowledged, all photographs are the property of Pearson Education, Inc.

Photo locators denoted as follows: Top (T), Center (C), Bottom (B), Left (L), Right (R), Background (Bkgd)

Cover DK Images; **1** DK Images; **3** Getty Images; **5** DK Images; **6** DK Images; **7** DK Images; **8** (TR, TL) DK Images; **9** DK Images; **10** DK Images; **11** Clive Streeter/Courtesy of The Science Museum, London/©DK Images; **12** DK Images; **13** DK Images; **14** Neil Fletcher/©DK Images; **16** (TL) DK Images, (B) Stocktrek Images/Thinkstock; **17** DK Images; **18** DK Images; **19** DK Images; **21** DK Images; **23** NASA.

ISBN 13: 978-0-328-39437-1
ISBN 10:   0-328-39437-8

Copyright © Pearson Education, Inc. or its affiliate(s). All Rights Reserved.
Printed in Mexico. This publication is protected by copyright and permission should be obtained from the publisher prior to any prohibited reproduction, storage in a retrieval system, or transmission in any form or by any means, electronic, mechanical, photocopying, recording, or otherwise. For information regarding permission(s), write to: Pearson School Rights and Permissions, One Lake Street, Upper Saddle River, New Jersey 07458.

Pearson and Scott Foresman are trademarks, in the U.S. and/or other countries, of Pearson Education, Inc. or its affiliate(s).

6 7 8   18 17 16

Suppose you are being driven to a soccer match, but your dad doesn't know the way. Today, that is not a problem. If your dad has a modern car, its tracking device will show him how to get there. How does this work?

Up in space a satellite transmits a signal. When a driver types a destination into the car's computer, it sends the information to the satellite. The satellite locks onto the car's position and sends back directions.

But what happened before there were computers and satellites? How did people find their way long ago? This book will explore those questions and more as we learn about the stars and how they help guide us.

Viewing the Stars

In good conditions you can see about two thousand stars with your own eyes. With telescopes you can see many, many more. Telescopes make it possible to see the stars in an entirely different way.

Stars are mostly hydrogen and helium gas. They are different colors, sizes, and temperatures. Their heat causes them to give off light. As a star ages, its hydrogen runs out. When this happens, the star expands and changes color.

Scientists measure the distances between stars in light years. One **light-year** is about 6 trillion miles! The star closest to our solar system is 4.3 light years away. The Sun, meanwhile, is only 93 million miles away from Earth.

STARS AND THE UNIVERSE

Stars usually revolve around one or two other stars. Often a group of stars will blend together to look like one star. Some stars travel through space in small groups of two or three, or in large groups of tens of millions. These large groups of stars are called star clusters. Even larger than star clusters are galaxies. A **galaxy** may include hundreds of billions of stars.

Some galaxies have shapes you have seen before, such as a pinwheel. Galaxies contain gas and dust, and are held together by gravity. Our galaxy, the Milky Way, is made up of the Sun, the planets, and more than 200 billion stars.

The Milky Way galaxy

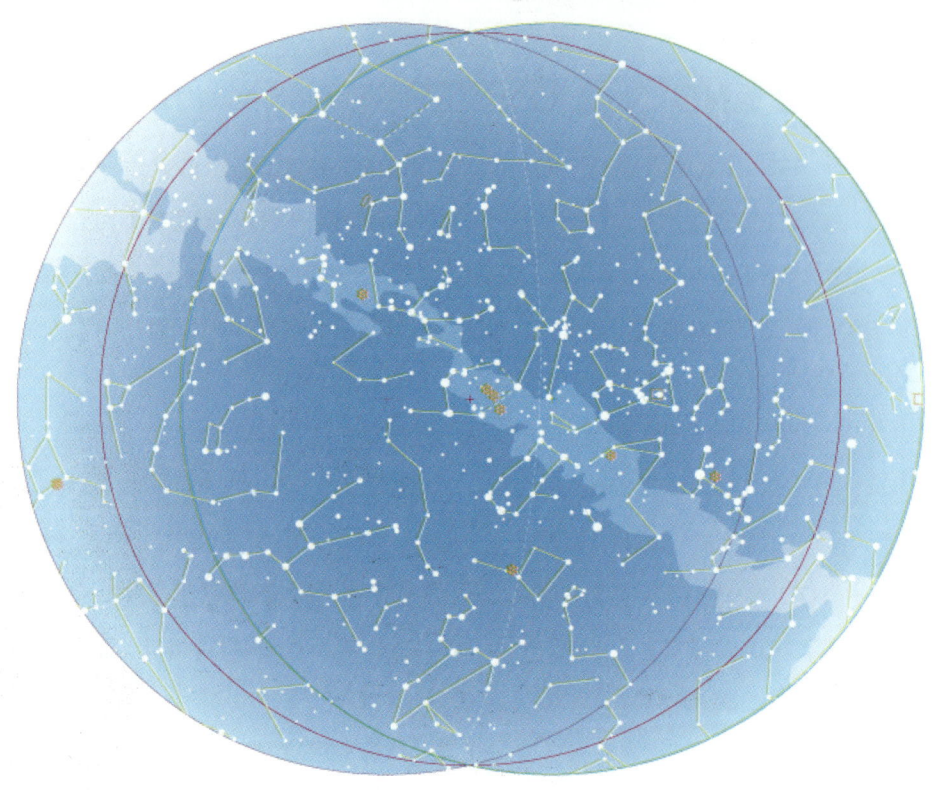

A chart showing many of the constellations

CONSTELLATIONS

Constellations are groups of stars that make up shapes in the sky. Ancient people named them after mythological creatures, such as unicorns. They also named constellations after gods and heroes from stories.

Astronomers are scientists who study the universe. They have named eighty-eight official constellations. These constellations are known to people all over the world. Astronomers from very long ago believed that the Earth was the center of the universe. They thought that the Sun, Moon, and stars moved around it.

Ursa Major

Ursa Major is one of the more well known constellations. It contains both a very famous star and a very famous set of stars. The famous star is the North Star. The famous set of stars is the Big Dipper.

A group of seven bright stars connect to make the Big Dipper. Directly above the two stars that make the far side of the Dipper's "bowl" (opposite the Dipper's "handle") sits the North Star. The two stars in the bowl are called the Pointers because they point to the North Star.

The North Star has always been the Northern Hemisphere's most important star for doing celestial navigation, because it is always found by looking north.

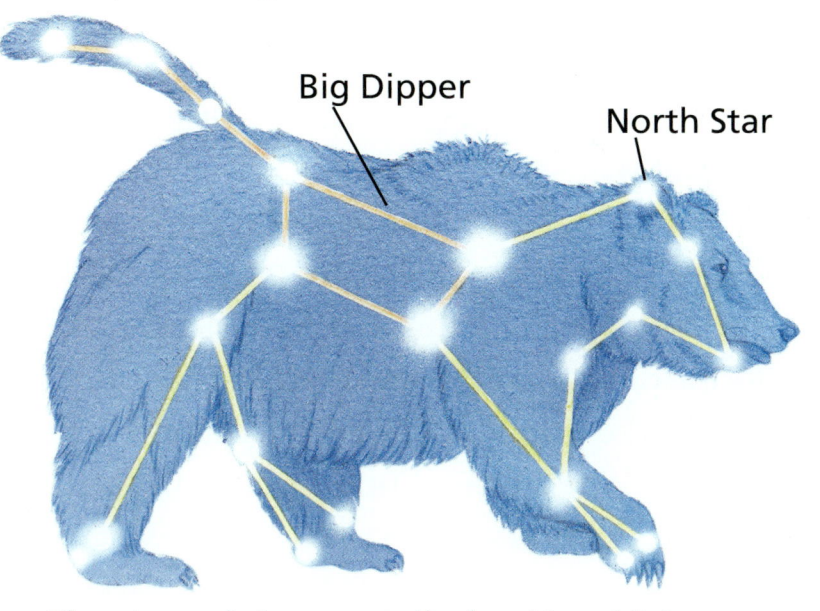

The stars of the constellation Ursa Major

Orion

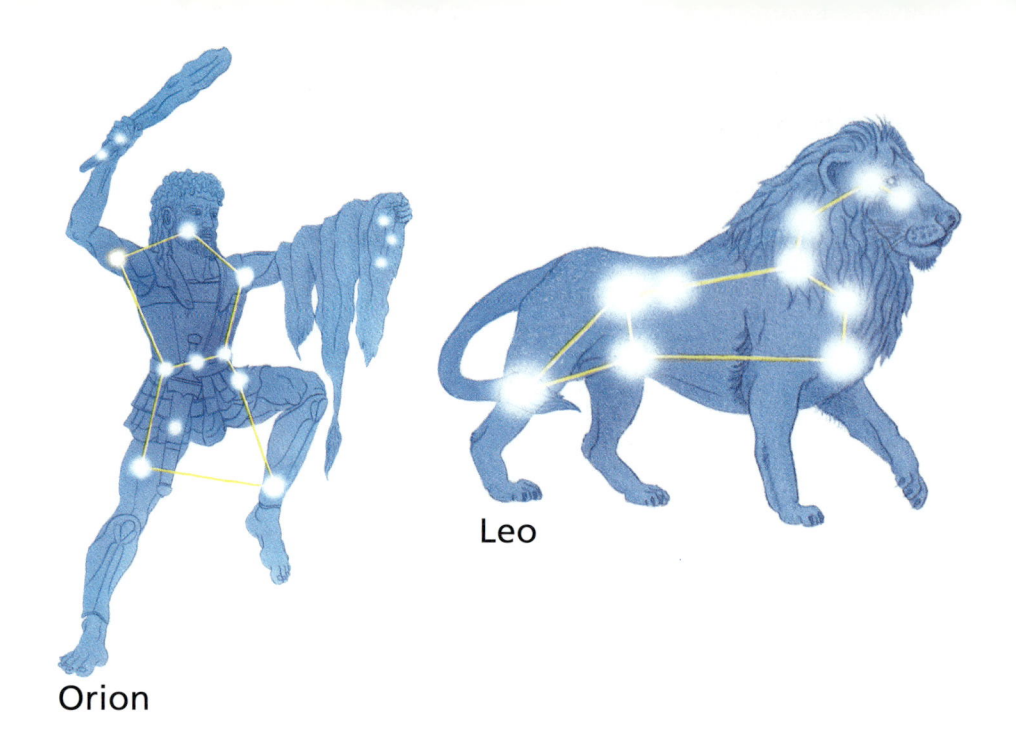

Leo

ORION AND LEO

The constellation Orion has more bright stars than any other. Some people think they resemble a warrior with a club, a shield, and a sword hanging from his belt. The belt is made up of three bright stars in a row. They are easily seen in the winter sky.

In spring, new constellations appear. Then you can see five stars in the shape of a backward question mark. They make up the head of Leo, the lion. Regulus is the star that marks the heart of Leo. To the left of Regulus are three stars in the shape of a triangle. The brightest of those three is the tail end of Leo.

Orion, Leo, and Regulus are just a few of the many stars and constellations that early explorers would have known about and used to figure out their location.

Of all the early explorers, Christopher Columbus is probably the most famous. He is known both for the places he sailed to and the different groups of people he met on his travels. But Columbus is also very important as an example of how early sailors navigated using the equipment and knowledge that was available to them. Read on to find out more about navigators like Columbus and how they were able to plot a course based on what they saw in the sky.

A statue of Christopher Columbus

9

EARLY EXPLORERS LOOK TO THE SKY

Finding your way without getting lost wasn't always easy. Explorers such as Columbus had only maps and a compass to help them. They had to rely on the Sun, the Moon, and the stars to lead them.

During the day, early explorers depended on the Sun. Because the Sun rises in the east, explorers knew they were sailing south if the Sun was rising on their left. If the Sun was rising on their right, they knew they were sailing north. But what did they do at night?

Think about what the ocean must have been like at night. After the Sun went down, explorers had only the Moon and the stars to guide them. That's why they looked to the stars and the constellations for help.

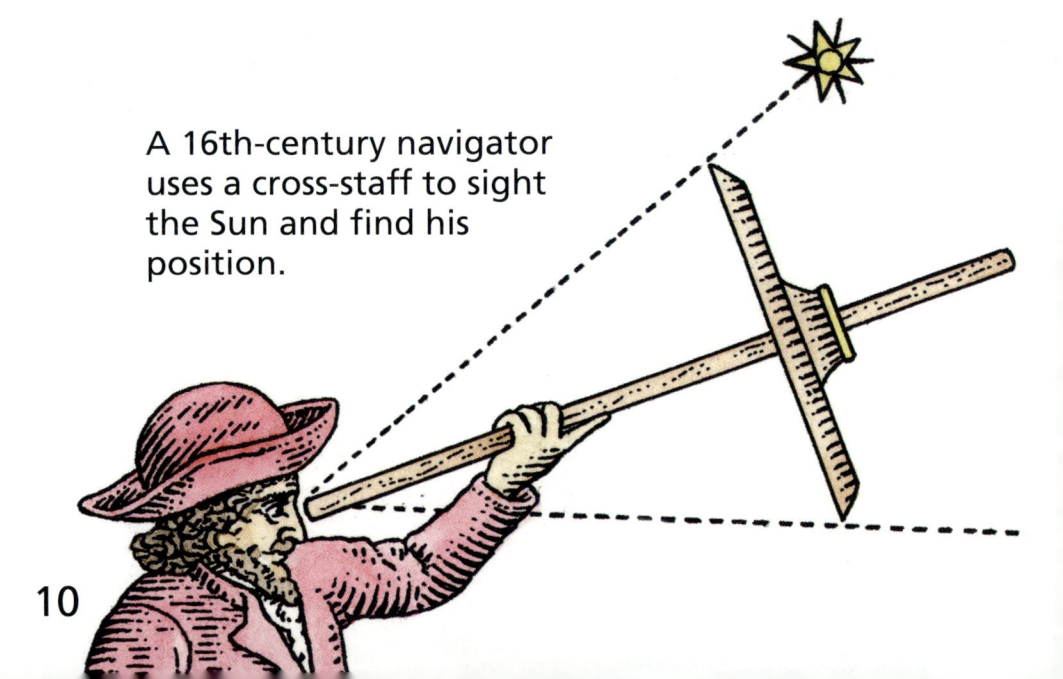

A 16th-century navigator uses a cross-staff to sight the Sun and find his position.

EARLY EXPLORERS AND NAVIGATION

A navigator is someone who charts a ship's position and course. All navigators need information about time, direction, distance, speed, and position.

Explorers like Columbus used a navigational technique called dead reckoning. With **dead reckoning,** a captain would start sailing from a known point and measure out each day's course and distance. Each day's ending position would be the starting place for the next day's measurement. Navigators used a magnetic compass to measure the course. They figured the distance they had traveled by multiplying the ship's speed by the amount of time traveled.

Early mariner's compass

COLUMBUS AND CELESTIAL NAVIGATION

Columbus also used **celestial navigation** techniques. Celestial navigation uses the Sun, Moon, and stars to measure latitude. Your **latitude** is your distance either north or south of the equator. Geographers draw lines of latitude from the equator to the poles. Fifteenth-century navigators measured latitude to help find their location.

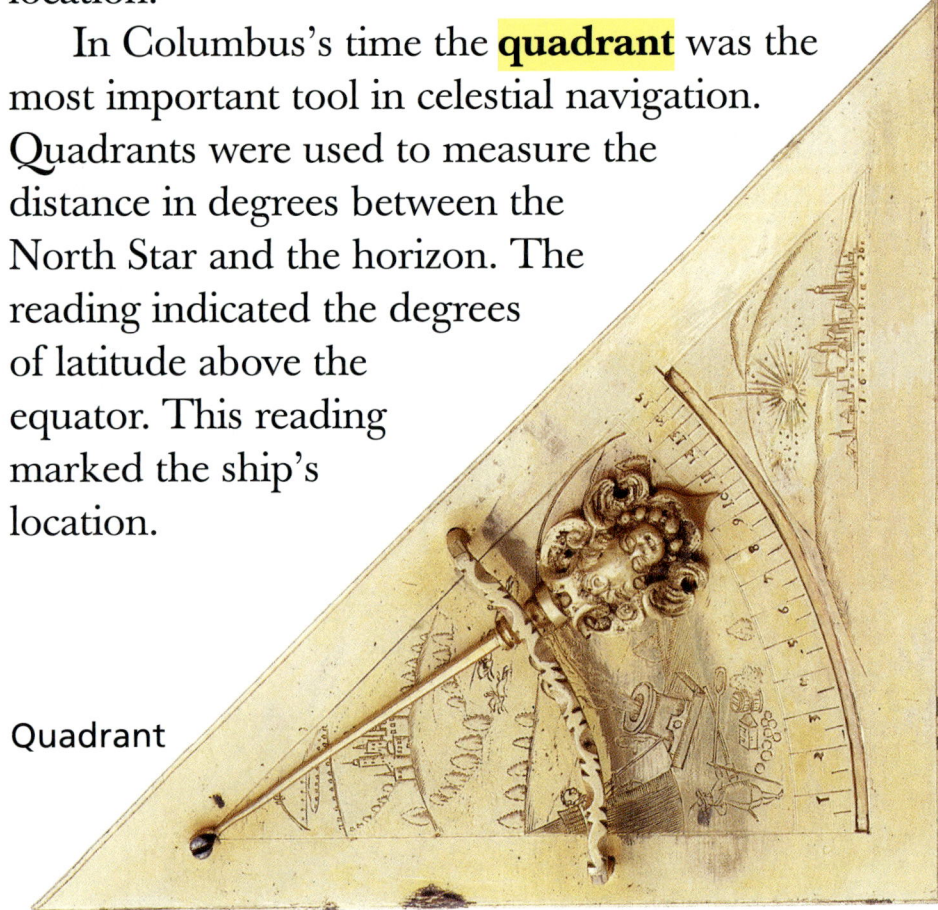

In Columbus's time the **quadrant** was the most important tool in celestial navigation. Quadrants were used to measure the distance in degrees between the North Star and the horizon. The reading indicated the degrees of latitude above the equator. This reading marked the ship's location.

Quadrant

Ocean waves make it difficult to hold a quadrant steady. The North Star is sometimes obscured by clouds. And the horizon can be hard to locate at night because of darkness. All of these things made celestial navigation difficult.

While explorers like Columbus were figuring out better ways to navigate, scientists were coming up with better ways to study the stars. Keep reading to find out about the new instruments that scientists used to prove their theories about the heavens. You will also find out how scientists borrowed from each other to come up with better equipment and ideas.

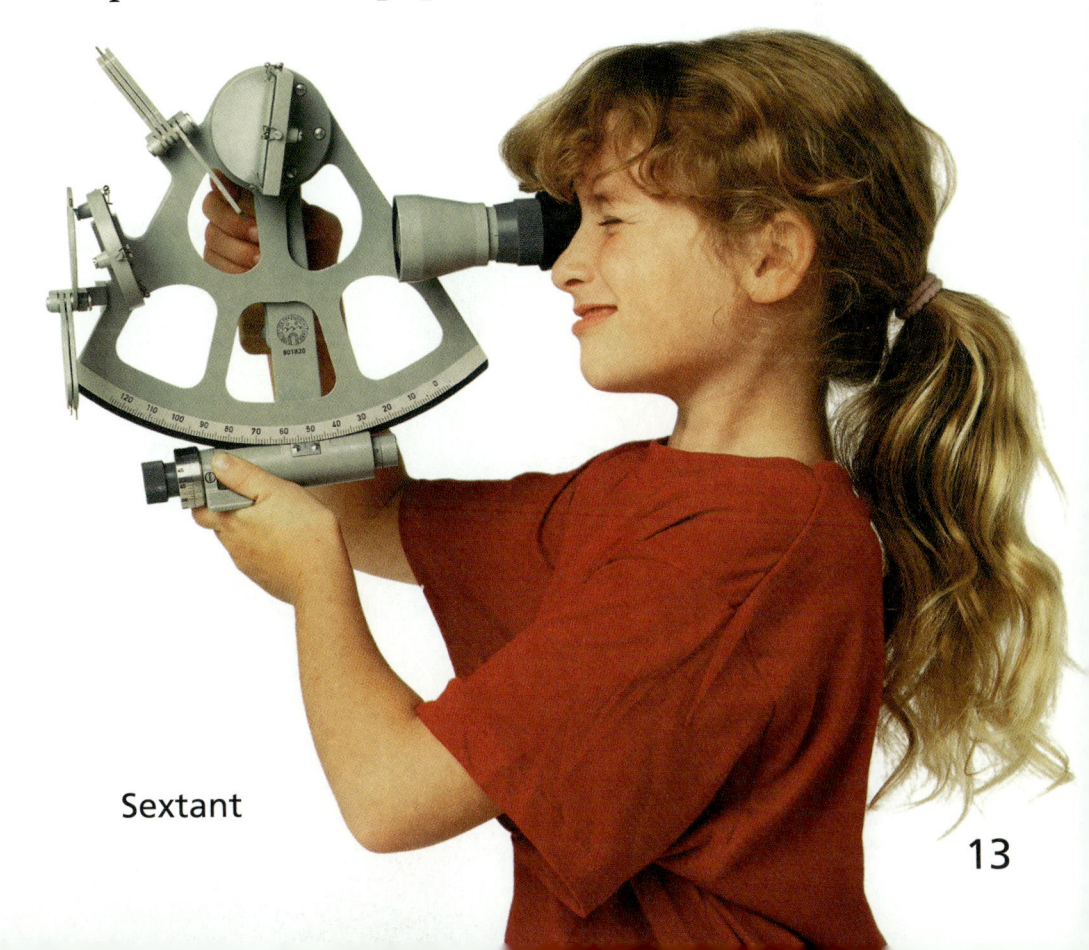

Sextant

A Scientific Breakthrough

The measuring techniques used during early expeditions were only somewhat accurate. Usually, navigators were off by a few miles. If bad weather prevented explorers from observing the sky, the results were worse.

Early navigators finally got help from three scientists: Nicolaus Copernicus, Hans Lippershey, and Galileo Galilei. That trio's theories and inventions would pave the way for space travel and exploration.

Copernicus was a Polish astronomer. He argued that the Sun, not the Earth, was the center of the solar system. Many people didn't believe him. Powerful groups challenged both him and his theory.

A Spyglass Becomes a Telescope

It took the invention of the lens to help prove Copernicus's theory. No one really knows who invented the lens. What is known is that eyeglasses were invented during the 1200s. It is thought that the inventor, while making windowpanes, noticed that he could see better while looking through them.

The spyglass was invented around 1600 by Hans Lippershey. Lippershey, who was Dutch, made eyeglasses. Some people believe that two children were playing with his lenses and put two of them together. When they looked through the lenses at a distant church tower, it was magnified. Lippershey supposedly used this discovery to create the first spyglass.

News of the invention spread throughout Europe. One of the people most interested in it was the Italian scientist Galileo Galilei.

Why Galileo Is Important

Galileo was already well known by the time he learned of Lippershey's invention. Galileo studied Lippershey's spyglass and built a bigger one. Galileo's spyglass made objects twenty times larger than their actual size. It allowed him to look at things in the nighttime sky that no one had seen before. He saw mountains, valleys, and craters on the Moon. He could see that the Milky Way was made up of billions of stars. Galileo's findings were important news, but some people refused to believe him.

An ink sketch of the phases of the moon by Galileo

Those people thought that the Moon was smooth and that Galileo was trying to trick them. To prove them wrong, he continued his observations.

One night in 1610 Galileo noticed four objects near Jupiter that no one had seen before. The next night, he saw them again, but in a different place.

What Galileo had discovered was Jupiter's moons. He was able to see that they were traveling around the planet. Galileo also discovered "stars" that circled the planet Saturn. Those "stars" were later identified as Saturn's rings. More importantly, Galileo watched sunlight move across the planet Venus. This proved that Venus traveled around the Sun, not the Earth. Copernicus was right! The Sun, not the Earth, was the center of our solar system. Earth was just another planet.

Replica of Galileo's telescope

GALILEO AND NEWTON

Galileo published his discoveries in his book *The Starry Messenger*. He also began selling his spyglasses. In 1611 a banquet was held in Galileo's honor. At that banquet Galileo's spyglass was renamed the **telescope,** which combines the Greek words *tele*, or "far off," and *skopos*, meaning "seeing."

Early telescopes allowed light to pass in a straight line from the front lens to the eyepiece at the opposite end of the tube. These telescopes were **refractive.** Their front lens bent, or refracted, light.

Seventy years later, an Englishman, Isaac Newton, invented a new type of telescope. Like Galileo, Newton was a scientist who was interested in motion and force. Newton's fame came from his discovery of gravity, but his new telescope was nearly as important.

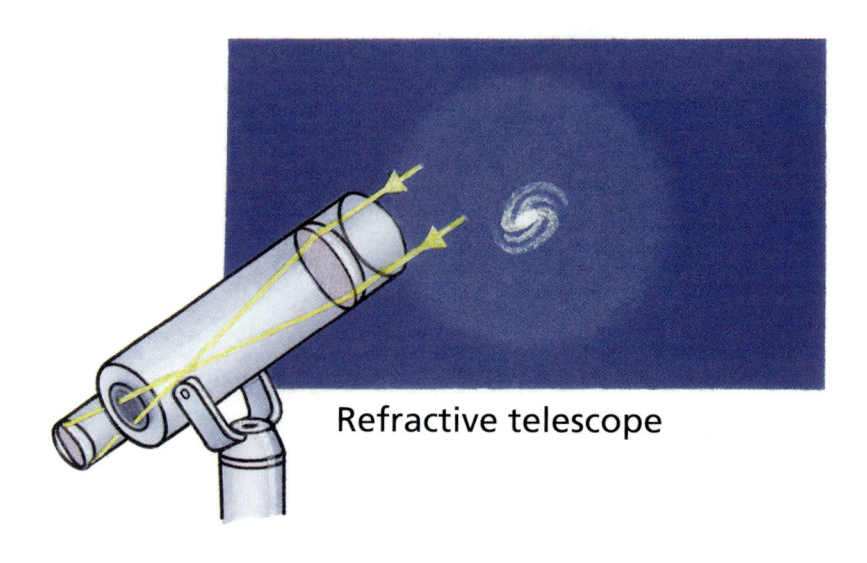

Refractive telescope

LATER TELESCOPES

Newton was interested in light and color. That interest led him to design a reflective telescope that used reflecting mirrors instead of lenses. In Newton's design a curved mirror was angled to reflect light through a side eyepiece. Shorter than Galileo's, Newton's telescope was much easier to use. Not only that, but its images were bigger and clearer. Astronomers would have to wait another three hundred years for the next big improvement in telescope design.

Reflective telescope

THE HUBBLE TELESCOPE

George Hale was an American from Chicago. From the time he was sixteen until his death in 1938, Hale worked to build telescopes to provide large images of the Sun. Hale eventually designed the 200-inch Palomar telescope. George Hale was a master builder of large telescopes.

Scientists continue to improve on telescope design. In 1990, NASA (National Aeronautics and Space Administration) sent a special telescope into space, named the Hubble Space Telescope. Its name honors the late American astronomer Edwin Hubble. The telescope has sent some extraordinary photographs of the stars back to Earth.

A drawing of the Hubble Telescope

You have now read about the stars and constellations, and where to find some of them. You have also read how early navigators used the stars to find their way. Finally, you have read how scientists used important new equipment to make discoveries about the stars. As you can see, people have been learning from the stars and using them as guides for a very long time!

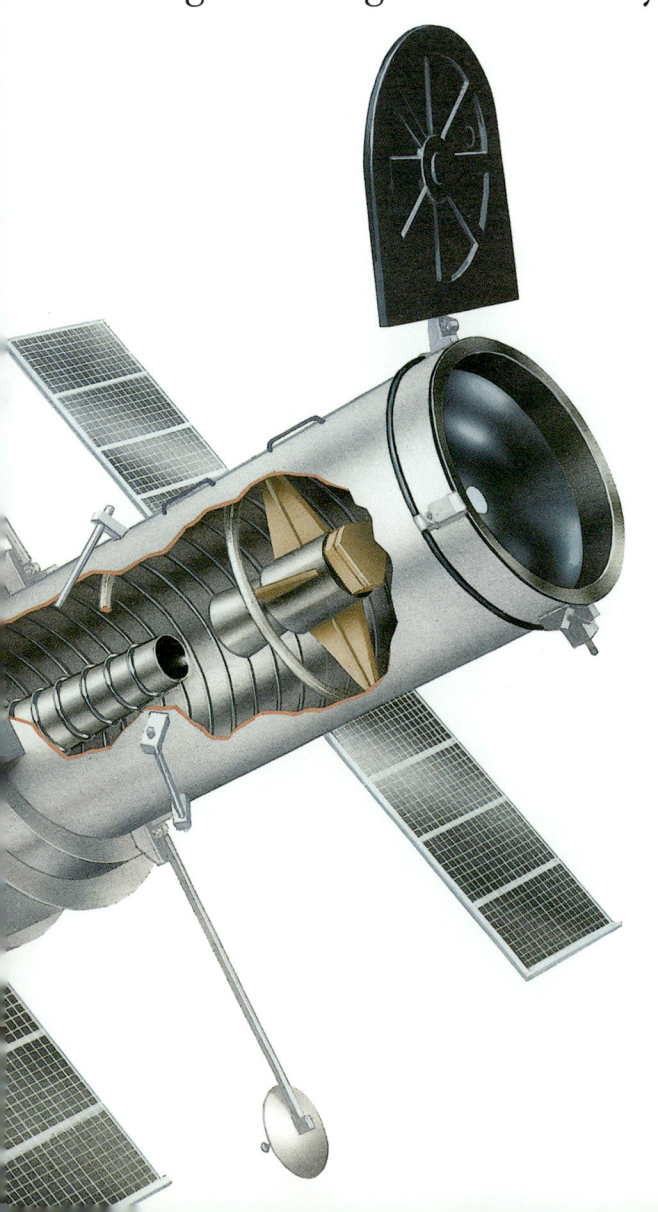

Now Try This

LOOKING INTO THE HUBBLE TELESCOPE

On page 20, you read about the Hubble Telescope. The Hubble Telescope is one of the most advanced telescopes ever made. It can take photographs of objects that are billions of light-years away.

Now, with this activity, you will be able to find out much more about the Hubble Telescope!

Here's How to Do It!

First, gather together in small classroom groups of up to five. Then, have each member of the group do research on one question relating to the telescope.

Here are some good questions to research: How does the telescope work? How and when was it launched? Why did it cost so much to build? What was the problem with the telescope? What has the telescope accomplished?

Once research on questions is complete, individual students may present their findings to the class. Have a notetaker summarize everyone's discoveries.

Glossary

astronomers *n.* scientists who study the solar system, our galaxy, and the universe.

celestial navigation *n.* a way to use heavenly, or celestial, objects to chart a ship's course.

constellations *n.* groups of stars that can be seen as patterns in the sky. There are eighty-eight constellations in all.

dead reckoning *n.* a method used by early navigators to figure out their ship's position.

galaxy *n.* a large collection of stars, gas, and dust held together by gravity.

latitude *n.* a thing's distance north or south of the Earth's equator.

light-year *n.* the distance a beam of light travels through space in a year.

quadrant *n.* an instrument used in Columbus's time to measure the distance between the North Star and the horizon.

refractive *adj.* when something causes light to be bent.

telescope *n.* an instrument that makes faraway objects seem nearer. Telescopes are often used to look at the objects in the solar system.